Unplugged!

the
bare
facts
on
toilets
through
the
ages

Anna Ciddor has always been interested in the lives of other people – past and present. When she became a writer in 1987 she discovered that her research gave her a great excuse to ask people awkward and intimate questions. For her books on the past she had to find out – among other things – how people used to wash and go to the toilet. This was such an intriguing topic she decided it was worth a book all on its own.

Anna lives in Australia with her husband and two teenagers. She has a studio at home where she can keep an eye on the washing, the cooking and the homework while she works. Occasionally, she escapes from her studio to give talks at schools.

Anna has written and illustrated a number of books, including: *Going Places: The Kids' Own Travel Book*, *Have Kids – Will Travel*, *Take Me Back*, *Through Children's Eyes* (a series of 6 historical books), *Christmas in Australia*, and the *Look Back* series (5 books).

Anna Ciddor

Unplugged!

the
bare
facts
on
toilets
through
the
ages

A LITTLE ARK BOOK

ALLEN & UNWIN

© Text and b/w illustrations, Anna Ciddor, 1997

All rights reserved. No part of this publication may be reproduced or transmitted in any form or by any means, electronic or mechanical, including photocopying, recording, or any information storage and retrieval system, without permission in writing from the publisher.

First published 1997. This edition published 1997
A Little Ark Book. Allen & Unwin Pty Ltd
Distributed in the U.S.A. by Independent Publishers Group,
814 North Franklin Street, Chicago, IL. 60610, Phone 312 337 0747,
Fax 312 337 5985, Internet: ipgbook@mcs.com
Distributed in Canada by McClelland & Stewart,
481 University Avenue, Suite 900, Toronto, O.N. M5G, 2E9,
Phone 416 598 1114, Fax 416 598 4002

ISBN 1 86448 454 3

Cover illustration by Leigh Hobbs
Text illustrations by Anna Ciddor
Typeset by Midland Typesetters
Printed by McPherson's Printing Group

10 9 8 7 6 5 4 3 2 1

Acknowledgements: the quote on page 34 comes from *Six Bob-a-Day Tourist* by Janet Morice, Penguin, Melbourne, 1985

Photo credits: Thanks to Catherine O'Rourke for picture research. Roman aqueduct: Coo-ee Historical Picture Library • China chamberpot: courtesy of Jean Price, photo by Catherine O'Rourke • Sanitary potter's advertisement: 'La Trobe Collection', State Library of Victoria • Backyard privy: courtesy of the Sovereign Hill Museums Association, Ballarat, Victoria • Airplane toilet: courtesy of QANTAS, photo by Mark O'Rourke • Japanese bath: Coo-ee Historical Picture Library • Soldier in Tobruk, 1941: Australian War Memorial, No. 040632 • The queue for the standpipe, 1863: Mary Evans Picture Library, London • Rat catchers in Sydney, 1900: Image Library, State Library of New South Wales • Water tanks in India: World Vision Australia • Nightcart: Museum of Victoria, Scienceworks Collection • Exeloo: courtesy of WC Convenience Management

Contents

1 Getting Flushed 7
A history of toilets

2 Getting Clean 21
A history of baths

3 Dirty Stories 37
The spread of disease

4 Pits, Ponds and Paddies 51
Managing without plumbing

5 Down the Plughole 62
What happens to sewage

6 Making Bubbles 75
Solutions for cleaning teeth,
hair and other bits

7 Care for a Dust Bath? 84
Animal hygiene

Glossary 93

Further reading 94

Index 95

This book is dedicated to all the students I meet on school visits.

1 Getting Flushed

A history of toilets

No privacy – *an ancient Roman forica, 2000 years ago*
Popilius strode into the room, his leather sandals slapping on the stone floor, his toga swirling. The *forica* was beautifully decorated with statues and paintings, and a sparkling water fountain. Around the walls there were marble seats.

Popilius called 'Ave' to several people sitting, chatting, then lifted his toga and sat on the seat next to his friend, Lucius. In the middle of each seat was a hole. Everyone in the room was going to the toilet!

UNPLUGGED!
Getting Flushed

> **DID YOU KNOW?**
> In Japanese public toilets there are buttons to turn on music so other people can't hear you go to the toilet.

Beneath the seats, a channel of running water washed the sewage away. Instead of toilet paper, Popilius used a stick with a sponge on the end. When he finished, he put it back in a jug of salt water.

No running water – *an English castle, 1132*

Elfrida shivered and hugged her cloak around her. Although it was sunny outside, no warmth reached her bedroom in the tower. The walls of the castle were made of stone and her window was only a narrow slit to shoot arrows through. Shivering, she opened the door to the toilet in the tower wall. It was in a tiny room called a garderobe, which jutted out from the outside wall. The contents of the toilet emptied down a shaft, then slid down the outside of the tower wall into the moat (the circle of water around the castle). When Elfrida sat on the cold stone seat, she felt a breeze blow up from below. Sometimes when enemies attacked a castle they climbed up these shafts and got inside through the toilets!

the toilet emptied into the moat...

Natural running water – *a village on the Fleet River, England, 1355*

Mary listened to the early morning village sounds: the bustle of people opening doors and windows, calling

"Good morning", clattering wooden buckets at the wells. But there was something missing. What was it? She helped her little brothers and sisters to dress, then they walked down to the river to use the latrine (the public toilet). There was no toilet in their little earthen-floored cottage. The latrine was a wooden bridge with holes in it that emptied straight into the river. There were enough holes for them all to sit together.

Now Mary realized why the village sounded quiet. There was no sound of running water. The river was so full of sewage that the water had stopped flowing.

Mary sent the little ones home, then threaded her way along the narrow cobbled streets to the shops, careful not to step in the smelly open gutter. Many people kept buckets or chamberpots in their bedrooms to use for toilets at night. They emptied these into the gutter in the morning. Mary was concentrating so hard on her feet she forgot to look up. A window above her opened and a deluge of warm liquid landed on Mary's head. Someone had emptied their chamberpot.

The river near Mary's house was called the Fleet River. At that time it supplied water to London! Centuries later, in 1841, people realized that the Fleet River had become a sewer, so it was covered over and is still used as a sewer today.

The bucket – *Edinburgh, Scotland, 1750*
Thomas worked as a clerk in a lawyer's office. All day he sat at his tall desk and wrote in a large record

UNPLUGGED!
Getting Flushed

book. This morning, as he dipped his quill pen in the bottle of ink, he wriggled uncomfortably on his high stool. He was listening, anxiously... Ah, at last, the loud call of "Who wants me for a bawbee?" (Who wants me for threepence?) Thomas dashed into the street.

There was the man, draped in a huge dark cloak. Thomas held out a coin. The man opened his cloak to reveal two wooden buckets hung on a yoke over his shoulders. He lowered the buckets slowly to the ground, careful not to spill them. Then, as Thomas undid the buttons on his pants to sit on a bucket, the man wrapped the huge cloak around to hide him from view.

The chamberpot – *grand household in England, 1750*

In his bedroom, Lord Marchant finished using his commode and ordered his servant, John, to empty it. (A commode was a toilet chair with a hole in the seat for the chamberpot.) Wrinkling his nose, John lifted the chamberpot out of the commode, carried it through the house, down the stairs and into the basement. Chamberpots were emptied into cesspools dug into the basement floor.

...cesspools in the basement...

It was a warm summer evening. Up in the main rooms of the house, maids were strewing branches of scented herbs on the floor and setting out bowls of potpourri. Twenty guests were coming to dinner, and the stench in the house was unbearable. Lady Marchant sat on a chair waving a fan and holding a perfumed handkerchief to her nose. 'I feel so ill,' she moaned.

John was glad to leave the basement and return the chamberpot. The commode seat was padded and upholstered to make it comfortable, but the smell had been absorbed into the fabric, which couldn't be washed. John hurried down to the dining room to finish setting up for dinner. When dinner was over, the ladies would retire to another room while the men sat around smoking and drinking. It was John's job to place a row of chamberpots on the sideboard for the gentlemen to use while they were having drinks.

A touch of class

The first chamberpots were made of rough clay, but by the 1700s they were made of fine decorated china, like plates and cups. Some of them had funny pictures or poems printed in them. One popular design had a big eye painted inside, and a poem:

Use me well, and keep me clean,
And I'll not tell what I have seen.

In those days, people traveled by horse and carriage. Private carriages sometimes had holes in the wooden seats, hidden by cushions, with chamberpots underneath. So you didn't have to

UNPLUGGED!
Getting Flushed

worry if you were caught short during a long carriage trip!

In the Palace of Versailles, in France, there were portable commode chairs. You could have the footmen carry you over to your friends so you'd have someone to talk to while you did your business. And men were allowed to urinate onto the passage walls! This made the marble floors, gold paintwork and fabulous tapestries rather wet and stinky.

The outhouse – *a settler's home in Australia, 1850*
It was raining. Georgiana hurried across the backyard to the outhouse. The door was made of wooden palings and had a gap at the top and bottom. Georgiana bent down to see if there were any boots visible under the door. No, the outhouse was empty. She sniffed the flowers growing near the outhouse, then opened the door. Squares of cut newspaper hung on a nail on the wall. (Toilet paper rolls were not invented till the 1880s.) The toilet was a hole in a wooden box, with a wooden lid. Georgiana held her nose as she lifted the lid. Under the box was the deep cesspool.

Squat style – *a Japanese home, 1850*
Keiko slid open the paper screen door and stepped onto the veranda. In white cotton socks, her feet made a soft padding sound on the wooden boards. In the

the outhouse

corner of the veranda was a box-like room made of wood, with paper screen windows set low in the walls. The toilet was a rectangular hole in the wooden floor with a barrel sunk in the ground underneath. Men came every few days to empty the barrel. Keiko slipped her feet into the pair of wooden thongs left ready, one each side of the hole. Then she squatted down.

The soldiers' latrine

In the past, soldiers had to dig a latrine: a pit in the ground big enough for several men to use

UNPLUGGED!
Getting Flushed

together. Roald Dahl, in his book *Going Solo*, described a latrine in East Africa in the Second World War. It was 6½ feet deep, 16½ feet long, and very wide. The 'seat' was a long round pole hung over the hole. Roald watched another soldier, to see how to use the latrine. The man pulled down his pants and took a backward leap. He managed to land his bottom on the pole, but then swung over and tipped off – right into the pit! Roald pulled him out, and decided he'd rather go in the bushes.

> tipped into the pit!

What modern high-tech hygiene equipment do soldiers use nowadays when they go into battle? A shovel!

The flushing toilet

If you'd lived in 1596, you could have met the first person to invent a mechanically flushing toilet. His name was Sir John Harington. He made one for himself, and one for his godmother – who happened to be Queen Elizabeth I of England. The toilet was a bowl with a plug at the bottom, set into a wooden box. Above the toilet was a cistern, or tank filled with water. To flush, you opened a valve in the cistern and water ran down a pipe into the bowl. Then you pulled a handle to open the plug and let the dirty water out.

Unfortunately, flushing toilets need a water supply to fill the cistern, and a sewer to flush into. Harington's toilet probably drained into an

> **HAVE YOU SEEN?**
> Some modern public toilet cubicles are so high-tech and automatic they just about go to the toilet for you! Water, soap and hot air squirt out automatically when you hold your hands in the right places. The door slides open automatically if you stay in too long (how embarrassing!). And last of all, when you step out, the cubicle automatically washes itself!

open street gutter. In the 1500s, there were hardly any water pipes. It was not until the 1770s, when piped water was more common, that people started to install flushing toilets.

From that time, inventors worked hard to make the perfect toilet. They had trouble making the flush strong enough to actually clean the toilet. A man called Thomas Crapper invented the syphonic flush which is still used today. It pushes a full cistern of water through a tube – a syphon – so that it comes out with high pressure. People say that the word 'crap' comes from his name, but it was already in use when he was a boy. Maybe he got teased about it at school, and that inspired him to do research on toilets!

toilets with painted flowers

Toilet manufacturers each tried to prove that their toilets were the best. In the 1880s a manufacturer called Jennings displayed a cistern with a glass front and goldfish swimming inside, to show how clean the water was!

By 1900, flushing toilets were made of

UNPLUGGED!
Getting Flushed

china, with painted flowers all over them – inside and out. The seats were polished wood. The toilet cistern was attached high up on the wall with a chain hanging down that you pulled to make it flush. If you were little, it was hard to reach the chain. (Some people still say 'pull the chain' when they mean flush the toilet.) The first flushing toilets were called Water Closets. The initials W.C. are still used for 'toilet' in England.

What's in a name?

Can you imagine saying 'wipe a drip-drip' instead of 'blow your nose'? So why do we say 'wee-wee' instead of urine, 'number 2' instead of feces, and 'go to the bathroom' instead of use the toilet? Many people are embarrassed to use correct names for some parts of the body and some natural body functions. The funny thing is that people from different times and different cultures are embarrassed by different words.

A hundred years ago, people in Australia and Britain thought that legs were rude. Ladies wore long skirts to hide their legs, and the sight of an ankle was considered disgusting. Even table legs were hidden under long tablecloths! Trousers could not be mentioned because they covered legs, so trousers were given names, like 'unmentionables'.

A euphemism is a word you use instead of

> ...the sight of an ankle was disgusting...

the real name. What happens after a time is that people start to think the substitute word is rude, and they make up a new name for the euphemism! Last century, the word toilet meant 'getting dressed' or a place where you got dressed. People were embarrassed to say they were going to the water closet, so they started to use 'toilet' instead. Today, people have forgotten what toilet originally meant. How many euphemisms can you think of?

Where does it come from?

Sometimes it's hard to find out where nicknames come from. There are two stories about the origin of the British word 'loo'. When people tipped their chamberpots out the window, they sometimes called out, "Guardez l'eau!" (French for "Watch out for the water!"). In England they pronounced this "Gardy loo". On house plans, architects used to call the privy (or john) 'le Lieu' (French for 'the Place'), and the English pronounced this 'Lyoo'. Does this explain why some countries call a toilet a 'loo'?

Have you ever heard a toilet called a 'boghouse'? That comes from the days when the toilet was a privy in the backyard. The cesspool underneath used to make the ground around the privy damp, smelly and squishy — just like a bog or swamp.

damp, smelly and squishy...

17

UNPLUGGED!
Getting Flushed

Spend a penny

Some English people say "I'm going to spend a penny" when they mean "I'm going to the toilet". The term 'spend a penny' dates back to last century when men had to pay a penny to use a public urinal (men's toilet). In many countries today you still need a coin to use a public toilet. Sometimes, you have to put a coin in a slot to make the door open. In some places, there is a toilet attendant who expects a tip.

Toilets on the move – Sailing ships

When thousands of emigrants went to Australia in the 1840s, they traveled in crowded conditions on small sailing ships. The wealthy had cabins of their own, and took metal wash jugs, basins and slop buckets on board. Some of them dared to use the W.C. – a wooden seat with a hole that emptied directly to the splashing seas below. Others used chamberpots, and sailors had to carry their stinking slop buckets past all the other elegant cabins to the shared W.C.

> water ration 1 pint per day

But most emigrants could not afford private cabins. They slept in bunks in large unventilated cabins below the main decks. Their toilet was a wooden bucket in the middle of the cabin, screened by a curtain if they were lucky. Water for washing and drinking was rationed to as little as 1 pint per person per day. It was stored in wooden barrels and became smelly and foul after a few weeks of travel.

Steam trains

The first trains didn't provide toilets for their passengers. In the 1870s, toilets were installed for first class, and by the 1880s all passengers had access to toilets. These toilets emptied straight onto the train tracks. Maintenance men working on the tracks had to watch where they walked!

Airplanes

On a plane, you can't have water sitting in the toilet bowl because it would splash people when the plane goes through turbulence. Designers have tried to make a toilet bowl that flushes clean without water in it. (If you've ever been on a long flight you'll probably think that designers still have a long way to go!) The waste empties into a tank and the toilet is flushed with a chemical solution instead of water (like portable toilets on a building site). Back on the ground, specially designed trucks pump out the tanks and sanitize them for the next trip. Tanks of water for handwashing are refilled. If there are any concerns about the hygiene of water in a particular port, the handwashing water is chlorinated.

Space ships

When you sit on a toilet on earth you can be sure that your urine and feces will drop downwards

UNPLUGGED!
Getting Flushed

> **ODD SPOT**
> In 1996 an Australian woman dropped her $75,000 ring down the toilet during a plane trip. When the plane landed, the cleaners had the revolting job of looking through the toilet tank for the ring. They didn't find it!

because of gravity. In space there is no gravity. If astronauts sat on a normal style toilet their excrement would rise up and go floating all over the space ship! To avoid this, they have a tube to vacuum away the urine, and evaporate it off into space. The feces are sucked into a spinning shredder, freeze dried, and packaged. Doctors inspect the feces like this when the astronauts arrive back on earth.

...freeze dried, and packaged

When astronauts walk around in space suits, they have a special container to collect the urine – but anything else they just have to do in their pants!

2 Getting Clean

A history of baths

The stone slab – *ancient Egypt, 4000 years ago*

Ancient Egyptians thought hair and beards were dirty. Men shaved their heads and wore wigs. Priests shaved from head to foot, and even their eyelashes were plucked out! They washed all over several times a day. When a priest entered the temple in the morning, he would stand before the statue of a god and announce, "I am a pure man." In ancient Egypt, most wealthy houses had bathrooms and people washed often.

Outside, the sun was fiercely hot, but the well-house was dark and damp. Senen wound her way down the curving steps to the well. She used a long wooden lever to lower the heavy earthenware pot into the well and raise it up again, full of water. Senen balanced the pot on her head and hurried to the house, where her mistress, Mentaret, was waiting to have a bath.

The house was made of mud bricks, but in the bathroom the walls around the bath were lined with limestone (mud bricks would wash away). The bath was a slab of limestone with a slight dip in the middle. Senen and the other servants helped their mistress to undress. They lifted off the long braided wig made of black wool that she wore over her own hair. They took

UNPLUGGED!
Getting Clean

off her rings, the snake-shaped gold bracelets coiled round her arms, and her necklace of large blue china beads. Mentaret knelt in the bath and the servants poured cold water over her, rubbing her clean with their hands. Senen was hot and sweaty and would have enjoyed a bath herself. Instead, she got even hotter, massaging her mistress with perfumed oils after the bath.

The giant bath-house – *Rome, 2000 years ago*

Have you ever thought of taking a hula hoop or a sword into the bath, or playing hand tennis in the bathroom? You might if you had a bath-house the size of a school, and you bathed with a crowd of people. That's what the ancient Romans did! Very few villas had their own bathrooms, so every afternoon the Romans visited a public bath house. (Men and women came at different times.)

> a bath-house the size of a school...

Popilius and Marcus were playing with a ball made from an animal bladder. All around the crowded courtyard, men and boys were playing ball or bowling, wrestling, fencing, or chasing rolling metal hoops. Marcus caught the ball, tossed it in the air, and said, "I've had enough, let's have our baths now."

The boys jogged past food shops and a library (the books were hand-written scrolls stored in wooden chests), and ran into the *apodyterium* (dressing room). Marcus placed his tunic and loin cloth carefully on the shelf, but Popilius dumped his on the floor.

At the door of the *sudatorium* Popilius asked, "Are you ready for this?" The boys plunged into the powerful heat of the 'sweating-room' and ran to the stone benches. The mosaic tiled floor almost burnt their bare feet. The room was heated by a *hypocaust*, a huge outdoor fireplace which fed hot air under the floor and up the walls. In a few minutes Popilius felt the sweat trickling down his face and running from his armpits. He nodded at one of the slaves standing ready with a pot of oil and a strigil (a metal scraper). Popilius lay down so the slave could clean him. He rubbed oil all over him, then used the strigil to scrape off the oil, dirt and sweat. Another slave cleaned Marcus. Feeling scrubbed, the boys escaped from the hot room and leapt into the refreshing cold bath of the *frigidarium*.

"How about a swim, Marcus?" called Popilius. Dripping and naked, the boys chased each other through the bathrooms and courtyards to the outdoor *piscina*. This gigantic swimming pool, 538 square feet (twice the size of a modern Olympic pool), was big enough for thousands of people to swim in together.

Roman engineers directed water from distant rivers to tanks in the city. They cut channels in the ground and built open stone pipes on high arched bridges, called *aqueducts*. Most water was fed into public bath-houses, wells and fountains. Slaves carried water to apartment buildings from wells or fountains. (The old fountains, with their famous statues, are still in Rome today.) Rich people

UNPLUGGED!
Getting Clean

could pay to have their houses connected to the water supply with lead pipes. The Romans didn't know that lead was poisonous. The word 'plumber' comes from the Latin word for lead – *plumbum*.

In the countryside, people got their water from a river or spring. They set up a statue or shrine where they could pray to the spirit of the river to make sure it didn't dry up.

The family tub – *an English castle, 700 years ago*
How would you clean your nose if you didn't have a tissue or hanky? How would you eat a bowl of jello if you didn't have a spoon? Modern rules of cleanliness and politeness depend on having the right tools. You've been taught it's dirty to pick your nose, throw your food scraps on the floor, or eat with your fingers. But in the past they didn't have hankies or tissues. They didn't have forks or spoons. They had dried grass on their floors instead of carpet. Things were different...

Alfred's governess read out rules from the etiquette book: 'If you blow your nose, wipe your fingers afterwards on your sleeve. At mealtimes, don't spit on the table, don't pick your teeth with a knife or clean them on the tablecloth. If you rinse your mouth, don't spit back in the basin, spit out on the floor.'

At dinnertime, Alfred went to the Great Hall and sat next to his sister, Marguerite. There were lords and ladies and many other children seated at the long table. A page placed a basin under their hands and poured water from a silver jug over their fingers. They would need clean fingers to eat their food without cutlery. They didn't have plates either – their food was placed on slices of stale bread. During the meal, dogs sniffed around the floor, waiting for bones to be tossed from the table.

Today was a special occasion. Alfred and his family were going to have a bath. The servants spent hours filling up the huge wooden tub, hauling buckets of water up from the well and heating it in an iron pot in the kitchen fireplace. Alfred's mother sprinkled rose petals in the water to make it smell nice. Then they all undressed and climbed in the bath together.

Sometimes Alfred's family went to visit friends in another castle. Alfred really liked the bath there. Their tub was padded inside with red cushions. When they got hungry, the servants placed a board across the bath, and served food.

UNPLUGGED!
Getting Clean

On tap at last! – *London, 1478*

2000 years ago, the ancient Romans conquered many countries, from England to Egypt, and brought them aqueducts and bath-houses. But then other people conquered the Romans. Time passed. The Roman aqueducts and bath-houses decayed. The world population grew. The water supply worsened. Hundreds of years later, Londoners were happy if they could get a little trickle of water out of a tap...

Ten-year-old John watched the workmen digging up the road to lay a water pipe to his house. No more paying halfpennies to the water carrier for the water he carried in the tall wooden container on his back. No more trudging home from the conduit with an aching back and a very heavy bucket. (The conduit supplied clean water, brought to town in hollowed-out tree trunks from a spring outside London.) Sometimes, when John was too lazy to go to the conduit, he scooped up water from a nearby well or ditch, but this water was polluted by the surrounding cesspools. Now, for five shillings a year, his family would have a pipe all the way from the conduit to their house, and a tap in their own kitchen! John was amazed to see how tiny the pipes were – just the size of a quill pen (a pen made from a feather).

(...water polluted by cesspools)

Suddenly he heard shouting and laughter around the corner. John ran to see what was going on. A constable was leading a horse and rider down the street. The rider had a bizarre hat on his head. It was a big pot with lots of pipes sticking out the sides, and water was spouting out the pipes!

> **DID YOU KNOW?**
> When there were public celebrations in old England – like war victories or coronations – the water pipes were connected to a wine supply instead of water!

"We caught this fellow connecting pipes to the conduit, without paying," said the constable.

The procession paused so the constable could climb up and pour more water into the pot hat. Water trickled down the face and clothes of the guilty man.

The Turkish bath – *a 'hummum', 1574*

In many religions, washing at certain times is a religious requirement. In a Christian baptism, the baby's head is made wet. Jewish men and women wash their hands before eating bread or after touching anything considered 'unclean', and women bathe every month in a special bath called a 'mikva'. In India, Hindus wash three times a day in the Ganges River. Muslims wash before prayer – hands, faces and feet. In the 1500s, Muslims in Turkey built bath-houses near the mosques to make washing more convenient.

A group of important-looking men were approaching the hummum. In their midst, swaying on a horse, was a

UNPLUGGED!
Getting Clean

short fat man, dressed in long robes of blue, red and gold. He had a long black moustache, twisted into two points, and on his head was a gigantic white turban. He was the sultan of Turkey, known as Selim the Drunkard.

Inside the hummum there were tiled floors, a tinkling fountain and the fragrance of incense. A wood-burning stove heated water that filled the room with thick clouds of steam. Bath attendants removed Selim's robes, and wrapped a towel around his fat stomach. They put wooden clogs on his feet so he wouldn't burn his toes on the hot floor. Selim clattered across to a wooden platform. A muscular bath attendant vigorously rubbed and pinched the flabby flesh and massaged his arms and legs. Then he scrubbed Selim all over with a rough soapy cloth. Another attendant wiped him gently with cold wet cloths. The steam 'bath' was over.

Selim was wrapped in a clean towel and led into another room to recover. He flopped on a couch and called loudly for drinks. Sweating in that steam room made him very thirsty. He was drunk by the time he stood up to leave. He tottered a few steps, then fell, smashing his head on the marble floor. Selim the Drunkard died a clean man.

You can still visit hummums in Turkey today.

The hip bath – *Melbourne, Australia, 1840*
In early Melbourne, water was scarce, expensive and not very clean. Families had a bath once a

week, usually on Saturday night. Baths were portable and made of metal. The most popular style was the hip bath. Some people had a shower bath. This was a hip bath with a pump you could work by hand to send the water up pipes to a tank over your head.

> a bath once a week

"Take this shilling to pay the water man, Isabelle."

Isabelle ran outside and lifted the lid to peer into the water barrel. She leapt back with a screech as a cockroach came whizzing out. There was only a thin skin of smelly water left at the bottom of the barrel, and it was dotted with dying cockroaches. It was a week since their last water delivery.

The water cart drew up and the driver unhooked the leather hose from the barrel on his cart. He slipped

UNPLUGGED!
Getting Clean

the nozzle of the hose through the square hole in the fence into their barrel. Isabelle climbed the fence rails to watch. The hose swelled up and gurgled as the water poured in.

Shyly, she handed the man his shilling. He swung himself up onto the cart, with a yell and a crack of the whip. The horse trotted off, back to the Yarra River where the man would pump up water to fill his barrel again, and make a delivery to another house. Isabelle quickly filled a bucket with the fresh water. She heaved it up and carried it into the house.

"Fill the kettle up," said Ma. "I'm dying for a cuppa' tea." The kettle was a huge black cast iron pot that hung over the cooking fire in the kitchen. Isabelle stood the kettle on the rough wooden table and took off the lid. She covered the opening with a cloth before she started to pour in the water. The cloth filtered out the dead insects and green slime in the water.

After tea, it was time to get ready for their once-a-week bath. Ma unhooked the metal hip bath that hung on the kitchen wall and stood it on the stone floor. Isabelle's brothers chopped wood for the fire, and helped bring more buckets of water from the barrel outside. Isabelle dragged the wooden towel stand over near the fire and hung the towels there to warm. When the bath was nearly full of cold water, Ma lifted the heavy steaming kettle off the fire and poured in the boiling water. Isabelle undressed the baby. Starting with the youngest, they would each have a turn in the same bath water.

Next time you turn on the tap to have a warm bath or shower, all by yourself, in the privacy of a bathroom with a closed door, think about how lucky you are!

Hot water – *bursting boilers in London, 1875*
Daring new inventions, like built-in baths and water heaters, could be dangerous...

The builders and plumbers had left and the house was peaceful and tidy at last. Mrs. Woodside opened a door and smiled with pleasure at the sight of her new bathroom. It had once been a bedroom. There was still flowered wallpaper on the walls, heavy curtains at the windows and a thick rug on the wooden floor. But instead of the bed there was now a glossy new bath and shining brass pipes. The bath was brown on the outside and painted to look like marble inside. It stood on little feet shaped like animal paws.

Mrs. Woodside turned on the tap (there was no hot water, just one cold tap). As the bath began to fill, she lit the coal fire underneath it to heat the water. She was glad that women were allowed to have warm baths. Mr. Woodside, like many men, had his baths cold. Warm baths were supposed to be sissy.

Mrs. Woodside climbed in, soaped herself and lay back for a soak. The water was getting hotter and hotter, and so was the bath. It was almost burning her. With a shock she realized she had left the coal fire on underneath. She was being cooked! She leapt out of the bath. Her skin was bright red, and the paint on the bath was melting off.

UNPLUGGED!
Getting Clean

Mr. Woodside called the plumber to bring a different water heater. In the kitchen he installed a big boiler, to be heated by the stove. He knocked holes in walls and ceilings to put in more pipes: a pipe from a storage tank in the ceiling to feed water down to the boiler, and a pipe to take hot water from the kitchen up to the bath.

It was winter. Snow lay thick all around the house. When Mrs. Woodside ran the bath, there was just enough water in the boiler to fill it, but no water ran down the pipe to refill the boiler. The water tank in the ceiling was frozen solid.

Meanwhile Annie, the maid, prepared breakfast in the warm kitchen. The copper boiler sat heating in the corner – empty. The morning sun began to melt the snow outside, and the frozen water in the tank started to thaw. A trickle of icy water slid down the pipe towards the red-hot boiler.

> the red-hot boiler...

Annie set out the breakfast on a tray to carry upstairs. Just as she stepped out the kitchen door, there was a huge explosion. She fell on her face, and the tray with all the pretty china flew up and smashed against the wall. People came running from all over the house. There were pieces of copper everywhere. The boiler had burst when the icy water had touched the red-hot copper.

The furo – *a Japanese bath, 1885*

According to the Buddhist religion, a bath cleans away sin and brings good luck. For hundreds of years, while the Western world went largely unwashed, the Japanese had hot baths in their own homes — at least once a day!

Akiko dipped her hand in the furo — the deep round wooden bath tub — to feel the temperature of the water. Almost hot enough. The water was heated by a fire in a little copper niche in the side of the tub. Akiko knelt down and added more wood to the fire. Next to the bath, she set out a scrubbing brush, soap and a bucket of cold water. She hurried out to tell Grandfather that the bath was ready.

Grandfather had his turn first in the bathroom. He undressed and, standing next to the tub, gave himself a quick wash from the bucket of cold water. He climbed into the furo for a few minutes soak. Ah, the water was just right — almost boiling. Now it was time for a real scrub. He climbed out and scrubbed himself with the soap and scrubbing brush. Then he rinsed off with water from the bucket. All the dirt and soapy water flowed away down the special slats in the wooden floor. Now for a final relaxing soak in the furo.

Next, it was Grandmother's turn. The hot water in the furo was still clean, because the soapy scrubbing was done outside the bath. Everyone in the family would be able to use the same water in the furo.

Japanese people still like to bathe in the traditional way, though nowadays their tubs are made of modern materials and not heated by wood fires.

UNPLUGGED!
Getting Clean

Battle baths

During a war it is not often easy for soldiers to bathe. In the First World War the Australian soldiers were fighting for many months at Gallipoli, by the beach. Some men dared to wash in the sea – in enemy range! One soldier wrote to his mother to tell her how the enemy 'has a nasty habit of distributing small lumps of lead at great velocity whilst you are bathing'. Fresh water was brought to the camp in containers, and rationed. Once a month the soldiers put a pint of the precious water in a shallow tin dish and washed up. They used the same water to brush their teeth and wash their clothes.

> a wash once a month

During the Second World War, the army provided jeep baths for soldiers fighting in hot dry countries. Bath-sized metal carts were filled with water, hitched to the back of a jeep and towed to the soldiers' camp. The water was left in the sun to warm up, then the soldiers took turns using it. Naturally, the lowest rank went last. Often some joker would start driving the cart around while someone was sitting in it having a bath.

A bath tub story – *ancient Greece, 2200 years ago*
Thousands of experiments and inventions have been inspired by water. The bath tub is an excellent place for a scientist to make discoveries. In ancient Greece there were many great artists, architects and scientists…

King Hieron sent for Archimedes, the most famous scientist in Greece. "I have a problem," said the king. "I gave a jeweler a lump of gold like this, and asked him to make me a crown. Now I am wondering if the jeweler stole some of the gold, and mixed in silver instead." He handed Archimedes the crown and the lump of gold. "Take these home and solve the problem," he commanded.

'Silver is lighter than gold,' thought Archimedes. He weighed the crown and the gold lump. They both weighed the same. 'But that doesn't prove anything. The jeweler could have added extra silver to make it weigh the same. If I could melt the crown back into a lump… it would be bigger if he'd added silver to it…

UNPLUGGED!
Getting Clean

But I can't destroy the crown. I have to find out if the crown is bigger without melting it.' The question worried him for days.

One night he was sitting pondering over the crown while servants prepared his bath. They brought in jug after jug of cold water till the tub was almost full. Then they carried in the three-legged pot of boiling water that had been heating over a fire. When they poured this in, the bathtub was filled right to the brim. Archimedes put down the crown and hopped in the bath. Water flowed over the sides. For a moment Archimedes stared at the overflowing water. Then suddenly he yelled, "Eureka!" He leapt out of the bath and ran dripping and naked down the street to the palace.

Proudly, Archimedes performed his experiment for the king. He stood a large jug inside a bowl, and filled the jug to the brim with water. Gently, he placed the crown into the jug. Water overflowed into the bowl. "We must measure this water," said Archimedes. "Now we will do the same with the gold. If they both have the same volume of metal they will both spill the same amount of water." He lowered the lump of gold lump into the jug. "The crown spilt more water!" exclaimed Archimedes. "It must have extra metal in it. The jeweler cheated you!"

3 Dirty Stories

The spread of disease

Don't read this while you're eating ...

People of the past didn't know about the existence of germs or bacteria: tiny living organisms that breed disease. They didn't understand that they were spreading disease around their towns with their leaking cesspools and sewage in the gutters. They had no idea that every ounce of feces contains millions of bacteria, which fleas, flies and rats carried from house to house. People didn't wash their hands after they went to the toilet. Doctors didn't wash their hands when they operated or examined patients. A hundred years ago, people were terrified of going to hospital. Half the patients died from diseases they caught in hospital.

In small towns and villages, the river was used for both water supply and sewerage system. People threw in garbage and dead animals. They built their latrines directly over the river. They washed their clothes in the river. Then they fetched buckets of water for drinking and cooking. In larger towns

> **DID YOU KNOW?**
> Up till 1929 some people believed that a cure for whooping cough was holding the sick child head-first down an outdoor privy!

UNPLUGGED!
Dirty Stories

further from the river, many people just dumped their dung in a big pile in the street.

In 1347, London smelled so bad, even inside the houses, that one man didn't realize his neighbors were piping the contents of their privy into his cellar. He only found out when the sewage flowed up the steps and into his house! In 1564, London Council made a law that people had to sweep the road outside their house in the evening, and wash it down before 6 A.M. with ten buckets of water – but nobody did. Laws were made against tipping chamberpots out windows, but people still did it. If you walked down the street you kept close to the wall, out of range. And you held a bunch of herbs or an orange near your nose to combat the bad smells.

During the plague in London in 1665, doctors made no attempt to improve hygiene. But they did design special clothes to protect themselves from the air and smells. They wore floor-length leather gowns and hoods which went right over their faces. The hoods had pointy snouts poking out the front, filled with herbs.

When washing was naughty

Early Christians didn't know that cleanliness was necessary for health. They thought that baths were an unnecessary luxury indulged in by people who paid too much attention to their own comfort. For centuries, Christians in Europe and America were discouraged from washing. The early American settlers in Pennsylvania and Virginia even passed laws to stop people washing. Anyone who bathed more than once a month would be jailed! An unwashed body was a symbol of self-denial and humility. The child martyr, St. Agnes, was worshipped because she refused to wash her face for eight years! (Can you imagine that happening to you?) In London, in 1812, the council refused to pay to have a bathroom installed in the Lord Mayor's house. In 1851, when the President had a bathroom installed in the White House he was criticized for wasting money on luxuries.

What a stink! – *England 1785*

Lady Marjoram was preparing for a ball. She sprinkled her clothes with lots of perfume so she wouldn't stink too much. She hadn't had a bath for a year. Her etiquette book warned her not even to wash her face,

UNPLUGGED!
Dirty Stories

because this would make her sunburn easily (and tanned skin was very unfashionable). She used a piece of dry linen to wipe her face, as the book suggested. Her hair could not be brushed because it was arranged in an elaborate hairstyle, built up on a wire frame, with artificial curls woven in. Today it was making her head very itchy. She had her maid poke around and kill all the nits she could find, then she tucked her white ivory scratching stick with the carved claw on the end into her pocket. Knowing that the B.O. at the ball would be unbearable, Lady Marjoram put on her special scent ring. When all those unwashed bodies started to warm up, she could open the little box on her ring and sniff the scented powder.

One of the side-effects of being unwashed was having fleas and lice.

Nit picking – *the village of Montaillou, France, 1300*
The people of Montaillou didn't believe in washing, and certainly didn't have special delousing shampoo. If a woman wanted to show that

she liked a man, she would offer to pick his nits for him! Daughters picked nits for their mothers and fathers. Nit picking was considered women's work.

Monsieur Rives, like all the men of Montaillou, grew a long beard and long hair. He thought the smell of his unwashed body was a sign of his manliness. He sat in the sun on the flat roof of his house talking to his friend, Monsieur Benet, on the next-door roof. As they chatted, their daughters searched through their fathers' hair and beards, picking out the nits for them!

A night at the inn – *England, 1550*

Tonight, Walter Williams would stay at the Laughing Head Inn (a hotel). He dumped his luggage on the bedroom floor and studied the room. There were lots of places where the fleas of earlier guests would be lying in wait for him. They'd be in the curtains around the four-poster bed, and in the straw and feather mattresses. They might even be in the tapestries on the walls. But Walter had a trick to catch them. In his luggage was a small bottle of hedgehog fat. He took a stick from the fireplace and smeared it with fat. He left this on the floor near the bed and went downstairs to dinner.

Sure enough, when he returned, the fleas had jumped to his bait. There they were on the stick. He picked them off, one by one, and cracked them between his fingers. Then he went to bed!

fleas lying in wait...

UNPLUGGED!
Dirty Stories

Battle for a bucketful – *London, 1820*
People couldn't wash, even if they wanted to, because clean water was so hard to get.

George walked along the street whistling, swinging his empty bucket. The sun was shining. The puddles from the chamberpots were drying out, and the paving stones were warm beneath his bare feet. He turned the corner and saw the long line for the tap. In this part of town, the tap was turned on just once a week, on Sunday, for five minutes. The water that came from the tap was not clean. Before use, it had to stand for an hour in the bucket to let the grot sink to the bottom. It was piped from the Thames river, but there were 200 drains that emptied waste into the Thames.

> let the grot sink

Just as George joined the line, the tap came on. People pushed closer and a woman dug her jug into George's shoulder. Then there was shouting. A man with a big barrel was hogging the tap and people were trying to pull him away. In an instant everyone was rushing to the tap in a screaming angry mob. George ran too, trying to wriggle his way to the front to reach the tap. But it was too late. The crowd turned away, growling and swearing. The tap was off.

George turned down a tiny lane and climbed slowly down the steps to his home in the basement of a terrace house. His father was breaking up a chair to light the fire. His mother was peeling potatoes into a black iron pot.

She looked up eagerly. "Did you fill the bucket?" He shook his head. "Then you'll just have to find water somewhere else. I can't cook the spuds without water."

George took a tin mug and went out to hunt around the lanes. At last he found a bit of water in a ditch. He tried not to think about where the water might have come from.

That night George went to sleep on his bed of wooden planks. The basement floor was coated with the smelly slime of sewage that leaked in from surrounding cesspools. The walls were grey with dirt because there was never enough water to clean them. During the night, George had terrible stomach cramps. He got up several times to use the toilet – the bucket in the middle of the room.

Even though he was only thirteen, he had to go to work the next morning. George and his brothers and sisters had all worked in factories since they were five years old. He needed to go to the toilet again, but the bucket was full, and there was a line for the one outhouse in the courtyard shared by all the families living nearby. George emptied the bucket onto the dung heap in the street. The heap was higher than his head.

Smelbourne, Australia

Early Australian towns were very unhygienic. In 1854, Melbourne was nicknamed 'Smelbourne'.

The bedroom door opened and Ma came out with a grim look on her face and a chamberpot in her hands.

UNPLUGGED!
Dirty Stories

> **DID YOU KNOW?**
> The average Australian family uses 170 gallons of water every day. That's because they can get as much clean water as they like – hot or cold – just by turning on a faucet. If they had to fetch water with a bucket, they might not use so much, and would have to carry one hundred bucketfuls to get 170 gallons! Today, there are still people in Africa and Asia who do not have easy access to water. In Sudan, each person has only 1¼ gallons a day.

"Don't you go in there, Edward." She closed the door firmly and marched out to the backyard with the chamberpot. She opened the gate and flung its contents into the lane. The whole lane was covered with stinking green slime and mounds of garbage. Flies rose in a cloud.

Edward believed it was the smell from this lane that had made his sisters ill with typhoid. He listened to the moaning and whimpering noises inside their bedroom. Would they die too? He could not forget the stiff cold little figure of the baby, Sarah. He ran out of the house and away.

A cart passed, crushing dry horse manure into powder. Warm wind caught up the powder, blowing it in his face, and in through the open front door. Down the center of the road there was a wide open gutter, running with the putrid liquid and brown lumps of sewage. Edward crossed the little wooden bridge over the gutter and turned down the lane behind the bakery. Today the delicious aroma of baking bread was overpowered by the odor from a cesspool overflowing into the lane.

People all over the world suffered from the lack of cleanliness. In London, in the same year, there was a terrible outbreak of cholera. In one district alone, 616 people died.

The discovery of bacteria

In London in the 1850s, most people carried their water from public wells or pumps. Looking for the possible cause of the cholera epidemic, Dr. John Snow examined the water supply. He found that all the cholera victims had been fetching water from the Broad Street pump. Then he discovered that a nearby cesspool was leaking, underground, into the Broad Street well. He ordered the pump to be closed down, and the epidemic stopped. Dr. Snow realized that something invisible was getting into the water and carrying the disease to the users. But what was that something?

something invisible in the water...

At his own expense, he published a book to tell the world about the dangers of this invisible enemy. People began to think that washing hands and keeping clean might be a good idea. Councils at last began to get rid of cesspools and install plumbing and sewerage.

UNPLUGGED!
Dirty Stories

Around this time a French scientist, Louis Pasteur, was studying a problem the French wine makers were having with their wine. Sometimes the fermentation process worked, and sometimes it didn't. Using newly improved microscopes, Pasteur discovered that the wine had tiny organisms growing in it. There were two different organisms. One made it ferment properly, the other made it go sour. Pasteur discovered that heating the wine killed the 'bad' organisms. He did some more experiments and discovered that nothing will either ferment or 'go bad' unless there is a tiny organism to start it off.

While Pasteur was making these discoveries, a Scottish surgeon, Lord Lister, was trying to solve a different problem. Half his patients died after surgery. He thought this was because the blood around their wounds was going bad, but he didn't understand why this should happen. In 1865, when he heard about Pasteur's findings, he realized there must be organisms getting into the wounds, making the body tissues rot and blacken. He tried the radical approach of washing his hands and instruments with carbolic acid, a poison which he hoped would kill these invisible organisms. It worked, and his patients survived!

The French silk manufacturers asked Pasteur to solve a different problem. Their precious silkworms were dying of disease. Pasteur discovered that the diseases were caused by microscopic organisms.

But what about diseases in humans? While he was doing his experiments with plants and animals, two of Pasteur's children died of typhoid. At last, in the 1880s, Louis Pasteur and Robert Koch, a German doctor, proved that human diseases, too, are caused by tiny organisms. Bacteria had been discovered!

Over the next few years, scientists discovered more about these mysterious microorganisms, visible only through microscopes. In the 1890s they discovered that people can carry bacteria or 'germs' when they are just coming down with a sickness, or recovering from it, and appear to be well. In the early 1900s, they discovered that fleas, rats and lice can carry germs.

Germ warfare

When you think of fighting a war you probably think of guns and bombs. But have you ever considered dropping a disease on your enemy to make them die? Long ago, armies would surround a town so that people couldn't get in or out. Then they'd catapult the bodies of cholera or plague victims over the town walls, so that people would become infected.

catapult bodies over the walls...

Germ warfare was still in use earlier this

UNPLUGGED!
Dirty Stories

century. The Japanese probably introduced plague-infested fleas into food supplies when they attacked China in the 1930s. During the Second World War, Britain and America also started developing biological weapons. By 1969, America had stocks of bacteria for several human diseases, as well as fungi to cause rice blast and wheat rust.

In the 1970s, eighty nations signed an agreement not to use biological weapons any more. However, there are suspicions that some countries are still developing agents that could cause diseases in humans, farm animals or food crops. They could easily introduce infected insects or animals, and spread something like the plague, foot-and-mouth disease or wheat rust in enemy territory.

The plague

The dreaded bubonic plague raged through Asia and Europe during the 1300s. In some cities, entire populations were wiped out. In 1900, the people of Sydney, Australia, were terrified when doctors realized one of their patients had the plague. By this time doctors knew that the plague was spread by fleas from diseased rats. They guessed that the rat culprits had traveled to Australia aboard a ship. The area around the docks immediately became a war zone – a battle against rats and infection. It also became a battle against the poor people who lived in the district.

The remains of a Roman aqueduct at Pont du Gard, France

China chamberpot, pre 1890

People line up for water from a standpipe, London, 1863

264

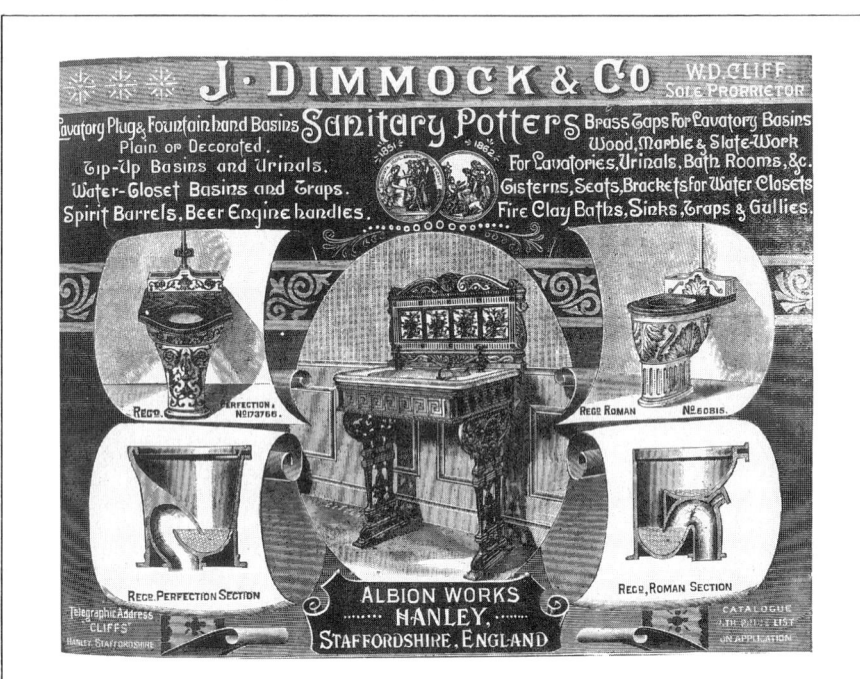

The backyard outhouse

A woman bathes in a wood-fired Japanese bath, 1930s

Opposite page, top Sanitary potter's advertisement, 1890s
bottom Rat catchers in Sydney, Australia, 1900

Emptying the nightsoil cart, late 1800s

Indian girls no longer walk 3¾ miles for water now they have tanks in their village

A soldier washes in a tin dish in Tobruk, Libya, during the Second World War: 1939–1945

Airplane toilets are waterless

The Exeloo self-cleaning unisex public toilet

Council workers from the Health Department went berserk with barrels of disinfectant and whitewash. They invaded houses, cleaning and painting everything in sight – even pianos and sewing machines were covered with white paint.

> ...a penny a scalp for plague rats...

People were kept in quarantine and not allowed to go to work. When the Health Department offered a penny a scalp for plague rats, the people grabbed this chance to earn money – in spite of the dangers. They tucked their pants into their socks, so the rats couldn't run up their legs, and armed themselves with sticks. But the fight was unfair. If a man was scratched or bitten by just one rat, or one of the millions of fleas, he would catch the plague and probably die. In fact, 103 people died before the outbreak of plague was brought to an end.

Good versus bad bacteria

There are more 'good' bacteria than 'bad' bacteria in the world. The bad bacteria have powerful poisons which can make us sick, even kill us, but there are also billions of helpful bacteria. They live in the soil, breaking down dead animals and vegetation to make the soil healthy, so new plants will grow. Without plants, there'd be no oxygen and we'd be dead! So most bacteria help keep us alive.

UNPLUGGED!
Dirty Stories

> **IS IT CLEAN?**
> Although people nowadays know that feces carry bacteria, many believe that urine is sterile. One fellow told me he washed a cut with his own urine instead of rushing to a tap. But urine can carry diseases such as worm infections, typhoid and paratyphoid.

4 Pits, Ponds and Paddies

Managing without plumbing

Imagine this ...

Guests enter a beautifully decorated room. The glass-topped table is laid ready with magazines, and each seat is actually a toilet with a clear glass bowl. The guests pull down their pants and sit on the toilets. They read their magazines and chat about things like how many gallons of urine are produced in the world every day. Then a little girl tugs at her mother's sleeve and whispers, "I'm hungry."

"Sssh," says her mother. "That's not polite."

Discreetly, her father goes to the maid and murmurs, "My little girl needs to eat. Can you tell me where the eating room is please?"

The little girl is shown to a cubicle. She goes in and locks the door. She pushes a button and a simple meal appears on a tray. Meanwhile, someone else comes and knocks on the door. "Hurry up, I need to eat."

This is a scene from a French film called *The Phantom of Liberty*. The producer of the film is pointing out that one natural bodily function is considered rude, while the other is acceptable in public.

UGGED!
, Ponds and Paddies

People in Europe, America and Australia think it is important to have private toilets, and sewage systems that remove our excreta far away where we can't see or smell it. Do you think this is right? In Asia and Africa, millions of people do not have such options, and use the age-old systems.

The long drop – Africa

Ibrahim lives with his parents, two brothers and grandparents in a mud brick house in a Nigerian village. The earthen streets around his house are baked hard and dry from the sun. Down the hill there are neat green fields, kept damp with water from the irrigation channels.

Ibrahim and his brothers don't go to school – they work in the fields. A few years ago, a community aid organization came to the village with machines, and dug a pit toilet for each family near their home. The pit had a cover made of sticks, with a hole in the center to squat over. It was scary to use, because the pit was 10 feet deep. (Pit toilets are nicknamed 'long drops'.) It soon became smelly and unpleasant. Ibrahim's family prefer to just squat down in the field. It's too far to go back to the house, and, in any case, in the field there is plenty of water for washing.

> ...pit 10 feet deep

Vietnam

In Vietnam it is always hot and humid. Nyen and his family live in a palm-roofed wooden house surrounded by rice paddies and fish ponds. They have easy access to water for the house from the irrigation channels. A few years ago, the government dug pit latrines near the houses. But when the monsoon rains fell, the pits flooded and feces were spread through all the houses. There was an

...cholera epidemic...

epidemic of cholera and lots of people died. The pit latrines are no longer used, but now they are a breeding ground for mosquitoes. During the day, family members go to the toilet on the ground outside the house, and urinate in the canals. At night, excreta is collected in a bucket to tip into the fish pond next day.

Paying the price

In Nyen and Ibrahim's villages there is not enough money to pay for sewage systems. They tried to change to pit systems, but, in fact, the artificial toilets brought disease and death to Nyen's village in Vietnam. Unfortunately, the traditional squat system is not healthy either. In Nigeria, the warm damp soil is a good breeding ground for the bacteria from the feces. Typhoid and hepatitis are common. When walking barefoot in the fields, Ibrahim and his family may pick up many diseases. Roundworm eggs spread everywhere, even on the vegetables which are picked and eaten raw. The eggs can be on the ground around the house where the babies crawl and play.

Unfortunately, medicines and health care are

UNPLUGGED!
Pits, Ponds and Paddies

not readily available to these people. Ibrahim's family is infected with roundworms and, in the gut, these worms steal the nutrients from the food. Ibrahim's mother is anaemic and can't work because of worms in her intestines sucking at her blood. One little brother is so weak he can't run and play properly. If he catches another illness he will probably die.

> ...medicines not available...

In Vietnam, Nyen and his brothers and sisters keep getting diarrhea. Last year the baby had diarrhea and died. From eating the fish and aquatic vegetables grown in the polluted fish pond, some of the villagers have become infected with parasitic worms, like roundworms or hookworms, that now live in their intestines.

Millions of people around the world today do not have access to a clean water supply, sewers or toilet paper. Their governments do not have the money to install plumbing and sewage systems. They cannot even afford to run simple health programs which could teach people about bacteria and how to boil water to kill germs. Because of this, many die of disease. In Africa, one in five babies die before they're a year old, and in Sierra Leone, health standards are so low that most adults die before their fortieth birthday.

Nepal

Nepal is a small country in the mountains north of India. In the city of Kathmandu people fetch their water from public pumps. It is contaminated because the clay water pipes and sewage pipes are old and leaky. People have to boil the water, or add disinfectant chemicals before they can use it. Most houses don't have sewers. Excrement is wrapped in newspapers and plastic bags and dumped in the street. However, only one tenth of Nepalese live in the city. The rest live in little country villages and work on small farms.

Joy Stephens is an English woman who lived for a year in a tiny Nepalese village. She described her experience in her book, *Window Onto Anapurna*.

In Nepal, fetching water is women's work. Joy takes a long walk downhill through the rice fields, following the sound of women's voices. Behind the spreading branches of a poinsettia tree, she finds a spring of water. The ground around has been paved, and here the women chat as they wash themselves and their clothes. Joy watches the women, some of them very frail and old, lift the huge water pots and carry them back up the hill. They put the pots in cone-shaped baskets which are carried on their backs and supported by a strap round the head. They wear a long piece of material wound round and round their tummies. This makes them all look pregnant, but at the back it provides padding for the water pot. Joy fills her own water pot, places it in her basket, then kneels down and tries to hoist it onto her

> women carry five pots a day

55

UNPLUGGED!
Pits, Ponds and Paddies

back. It's so heavy she can't stand up! The other women laugh and show her how to start with the pot on a ledge instead of the ground. This time, water spilling and knees buckling, Joy manages to get moving. By the time she reaches home, the pot is half empty and Joy has soaking clothes and a sore back. She feels humiliated when she sees another woman arrive back carrying two pots *and* a five-year-old boy! Most of the women carry five pots a day. Joy learns to manage with a lot less!

In the dry season, the spring dries up to a muddy hole, breeding flies and mosquitoes. The journey to fetch water is even longer. The children in the village go for days without washing, to save water. Any sores they get become infected from the dirt and flies.

The next task Joy has to learn is how to wash herself. There is no private bathing place. The women go down to the spring and wash under their long skirts without getting undressed.

But the biggest hurdle to overcome is going to the toilet. The villagers have chosen a bamboo grove, away from the houses, to use as a communal toilet. It is always full of flies and smells and people squatting. There is no privacy. In the monsoon season, heavy rain washes the excrement down from this grove to the rivers, polluting all the water supply. The Nepalese always wash their bottoms after defecating, so everyone carries a little metal pot of water when they visit the bamboo grove. The right hand is always kept clean, and used for eating.

Bangladesh

Ahmed takes a running leap into the pond and vanishes down into the water. He bobs up again a moment later, and squirts a high spout of water out of his mouth. Grinning and splashing, he dives under again, chasing his friends. A little girl squats on the bank, using the pond as a toilet. When she's finished, she dips in her hand and scoops up water to wash her bottom. None of the children take any notice; this is how they all go to the toilet. When the little girl is older, she will help the women to fetch buckets of water from the same pond. In the village there is a well which was dug by an international organization. The women used that when it was new, but they didn't like the different taste of the water. When the pump broke, no one fixed it. They are happy using the pond water.

UNPLUGGED!
Pits, Ponds and Paddies

In the cities of Bangladesh, traditional Muslim women often cover their faces with veils. In villages, religious rules are observed even more strictly. Women can only come out of their homes very early in the morning, before the sun is up. This is when they fetch the water and go to the toilet in the fields. If they need to defecate during the day, they can't. They have to hang on till dark, when they can go outside again.

In Dacca, the capital city of Bangladesh, there are no public toilets. Men and children just squat in the street. Five times a day, before they say their prayers, the men bathe with the holy water of the Ganges river. As the weather is so hot in Bangladesh, they pour buckets of water over themselves, clothes and all, or dive into the water. The water in this river is so polluted, visitors say it is almost solid enough to hold a stick upright.

no public toilets...

Bhutan

Jigmi lives in a village in Bhutan, a tiny country in the Himalayan mountains between India and China. His home, made from blocks of earth, stones and timber, has a pretty sloping roof and intricate timber decorations. There are mountains all around, covered with snow all year. The winters are freezing, and in summer, bears prowl round the house. The house is several stories high. The ground floor is the stable where the pigs, cows and horses live. To reach the living rooms, Jigmi climbs up a steep ladder. The toilet is a hole in the wooden floor of the front balcony. Jigmi wipes himself with a twig, then drops that down the hole too. This is a drop toilet, not a flushing toilet. There is no jug of water for washing, and no pit. The toilet empties straight down to the pig pen under the house, and pigs and rats eat the dung.

At Jigmi's school they have built a 'flushing' toilet. It is a pan set into the floor and the 'flush' is a jug of water. The children are supposed to place their feet in the special foot-shaped holes, and squat down over the pan. The jug of water is for washing bottoms, as well as flushing. There is a pipe running from the pan to an underground pit. When the pit is full, the drainpipe will be re-directed to another pit. But this toilet is a disaster. Jigmi and his friends are used to wiping themselves with twigs, and they don't know what to do with the jug of water. The twigs clog up the drain and the sewage is not flushed away. The pan overflows all over the floor!

Solving the problem

There are many organizations, like UNICEF, who are trying to improve world health by providing clean water supplies and toilet systems. This is a mammoth job. As well as finding the money, machinery and materials, they have to work out a system that will fit in with all the different habits and religious requirements.

It's no use providing different toilet systems if people don't know how to use them. Flushing toilets work if people wash themselves clean or

UNPLUGGED!
Pits, Ponds and Paddies

use toilet paper (which doesn't clog drains). But in many countries people can't afford toilet paper. In Bhutan the cost of one roll of toilet paper is half a day's wages. In countries where people wipe their bottoms with grass, banana leaves, twigs, corn cobs, mudballs or stones, a flushing toilet won't work.

One solution which has been introduced in some villages in Vietnam is the 'double vault latrine'. It is in a concrete building and it has two squatting holes and two collection boxes or 'vaults'. Only one is used at a time. When you squat, the feces drop down the hole into one concrete box, which is lined with soil. The urine runs along a groove in the floor to a pot at the back of the hut, so it can be taken away, mixed with water and used as fertilizer. When you finish squatting, you wipe yourself with something dry like leaves or toilet paper. Then you sprinkle two bowls of ashes down the hole to take away the smell and make it less attractive to flies.

When one box is nearly full, it is topped up with earth and sealed, and the other vault is used instead. The soil helps the feces to decompose. After a couple of months the contents of the concrete box can safely be used for compost.

> ...can be used for compost

The double vault latrine is relatively cheap to construct. It is suitable for drought areas because no water is used. It works well in hot countries where people traditionally wipe their bottoms rather than washing. Hot temperatures are needed to help the feces decompose in the vault, and the contents must be kept dry so mosquitoes don't breed. The double vault latrine is also used in Guatemala, with a moveable seat over the hole.

In countries where people like to wash after defecating, they need a toilet system which can cope with water. In some parts of India they use a double-pit pour-flush latrine. Instead of just a hole, the toilet is an in-ground pan with water at the bottom. The water is held in the pan by a curved pipe. After using the toilet, you flush it by pouring in a jug of water. This pushes the dirty water up over the curve of the pipe and down a drain. The drain is Y-shaped and connected to two deep underground pits. One pit is used at a time. When it is full, the waste is redirected to the other pit. By the time the first pit is needed again, about three or four years later, the contents look and smell like normal garden compost — safe to empty out and use as fertilizer.

Because these toilets have a pit design, they have to be carefully located. They cannot be in areas that are likely to flood. They must not be dug near water supplies, because germs from the feces could soak through the soil and into the water.

UNPLUGGED!

5 Down the Plughole

What happens to sewage

Take it away!

When cesspools were in use in Australia and Britain, men were paid to empty the cesspools when they were full. They did this with buckets and shovels. How would you like a job like that? In modern Japan and Taiwan some houses have sealed underground cesspools. Once a fortnight a special truck comes along, pumps out the cesspool and takes the sewage away.

In the late 1800s, Australians started to use pans instead of cesspools, and councils employed nightmen to empty them. The large, bucket-shaped metal pans were nicknamed 'thunderboxes' because of the noise they made when you used them.

> ...metal thunderboxes...

The night brigade – *Melbourne, Australia, 1870*

Once a week, Ruth was woken by the clip-clop of a horse's hooves and the rumble of cartwheels down the lane behind the house. On warm nights, the stink of the nightcart drifted in through the open window. She listened to the nightman as he opened the little gates at the back of each outhouse and dragged out the pans. There was a plop as he emptied each pan into his cart and a clang as he returned the dirty pan to the outhouse. Full pans were very heavy. As well as holding feces and urine, they were covered with sand, earth or ashes to muffle the smell. Ashes were best. When the night man tipped up the pan, ashes helped stop the dung sticking to the sides. In wealthy suburbs, nightmen were paid extra to clean and disinfect the pans before returning them.

The nightmen were supposed to drive out to the country to sell the 'nightsoil' to farmers. But many collectors in the inner city suburbs couldn't be bothered going that far. They secretly dumped their loads into the river.

UNPLUGGED!
Down the Plughole

Because the pans were sloppy and messy, they often got spilled in the streets. In 1878 a man called Hugh Bell tried to solve this problem by inventing toilet seats that separated urine and feces. The child's seat had a sieve over the pan. Women could use the sieve, or try to use the man's seat, which had one pan at the back for feces, and a separate one in the front for urine. This way the urine could be poured onto the ground or emptied down the drain. Bell suggested mixing the dry feces from the pan or sieve with dust and ashes and selling it as fertilizer.

> spilled in the streets...

Eventually, by the end of the nineteenth century, with the invention of flushing toilets and the improved water supply, councils in Australia and other countries decided to build underground sewer systems.

Where there's smoke

Up till the 1920s, plumbing was unreliable and pipes usually leaked. In bathrooms, people had to keep waterproof mats under their baths, basins and toilets. But it was the hidden pipes that caused more dangerous problems. Sewage could leak from sewer pipes into water pipes. Bad smells around the house were a clue that sewer pipes were leaking. To find the weak spots, plumbers put smoke, or strongly smelling oil of peppermint, down the toilet. It would leak out where there were cracks in the pipes.

Modern sewage treatment

Sewerage pipes collect all the waste water from bathrooms, kitchens, laundries and toilets. In some countries the pipes empty this mixture directly into rivers or seas, spreading pollution. But in places like America, most pipes lead to a sewage treatment plant.

Sewage treatment uses good bacteria to eat and digest the sewage, getting rid of harmful bacteria. The sewage is pumped into large settling tanks. It sits there till the heavy stuff, called sludge, sinks to the bottom. The good bacteria start to break down the sludge. The liquid – now called effluent – travels to another treatment area where it is slowly filtered through grass, earth or pebbles. Some evaporates. Bacteria eats up floating bits in the remaining effluent. The sludge goes to different tanks where more bacteria continue to digest it.

At the Werribee sewage 'farm' in Victoria, Australia, cows and sheep graze on the well-fertilized grass. The farm is recognized worldwide as a bird's paradise – for 200 different species. There are birds that migrate to Werribee every year from as far away as Siberia.

(...birds migrate to sewage farm...)

Recycling sewage

As the world's population gets larger and larger, we must recycle materials so we don't use all our

UNPLUGGED!
Down the Plughole

> **AWFUL ODD SPOT**
> How would you like to crawl into a sewer pipe and clean it out? In India, many children have to work instead of going to school. In Bombay, children are employed to clean and mend the old narrow sewer pipes. This job is not just unpleasant, the children who do it can become ill and die.

natural resources. We also need to save land for growing food, and cut down pollution. Does your family save glass and plastic bottles for recycling? Do you put out newspapers for the paper collection? Is it possible that we can even recycle the stuff we flush down our toilets?

In one week, an adult produces about 2.2 pounds of feces and 2 gallons of urine. People of the past discovered ways to put these to good use.

Cloth manufacturers used human urine to clean and bleach the cloth they were making. In ancient Rome, to collect urine, clay pots were placed outside shops for men to urinate into. In Britain in the 1700s and 1800s, cloth manufacturers actually paid people to collect their own urine in large pots. Once a week these pots were collected in special carts.

Gunpowder was invented in the 1500s, and urine provided saltpetre – one of the essential ingredients! In those days poor people didn't own chamberpots, so at night they just urinated on the earthen floor near their beds. In the soil, the urine formed into crystals of potassium nitrate, or saltpetre. The 'petre men' used to dig up the floors of their cottages to get the saltpetre for making gunpowder.

Soldiers in the Second World War found another use for urine. Leslie Poidevin, in his book *Samurais and Circumcisions*, describes how Australian soldiers made soap in a Japanese prisoner of war camp. The main ingredients for soap are fat and alkali. At the Glodok jail, the prisoners had to do butchering, so they could get hold of plenty of animal fat. The problem was getting an alkali to mix with it. Someone suggested using human urine. This was

...soap made with urine...

hunting for valuables

UNPLUGGED!
Down the Plughole

collected from other camps in 44-gallon drums and taken to Glodok. The soap made with the urine was so good even the Japanese used it!

In Britain last century, some people were so desperately poor that they used to hunt in sewer pipes for valuables. They climbed in and crawled through the sewage, hoping to find something precious thrown out by mistake, or coins washed in from a street gutter.

A good fertilizer

In China, people have fertilized their vegetables with human manure for thousands of years. Many Chinese migrated to Australia during the goldrushes of the 1850s...

Arthur was helping his father to dig, but stopped to stare in amazement at the line of strange people heading towards the goldfield. Each man had a long pole balanced on his shoulder, with bundles dangling from each end. They wore the widest, flattest straw hats Arthur had ever seen; wide jackets and short baggy trousers; and their shoes had wooden soles. But as they drew closer, Arthur saw the most curious thing – their hair hung in long black pigtails down their backs! "Chinese!" sneered his father.

The white golddiggers didn't like these 'different' people. They complained about the smell of their dried fish, about the way they took water from the water holes for their vegetable gardens, about the fact that the Chinese couldn't speak English.

One night, Arthur's father and friends were round the campfire drinking booze (bought illegally from the 'tea tent'), when a big angry golddigger rushed up bellowing, "Have you heard the latest? Those filthy yellow devils are using their own shit on their vegetable gardens." Drunk and enraged, the men grabbed knives and sticks and charged across the diggings to attack the Chinese camp. Arthur huddled by the fire, terrified, as tents went up in flames and the screams of the Chinese sounded over the goldfields.

In modern China, human waste is still used as fertilizer in country areas, though it is carefully treated to remove germs. When people go to the toilet, they let the urine run away in a groove, or into a separate container. The feces are collected in a shallow pit or a pretty wooden lacquered bucket. Using buckets, baskets or specially designed tricycles, people deliver their feces to the nearest compost station for recycling. A common procedure at the compost station is to make a mound of human feces, animal dung, soil and street sweepings mixed together. This mound is covered with a coating of soil with a little bit of manure mixed in. The coating keeps rain out and heat in. In summer, the compost temperature can reach 140°F, and the compost is ready to use in twenty days.

...faeces for fertilizer

Nowadays, there are many people around the world who make use of feces for fertilizer.

69

UNPLUGGED!
Down the Plughole

Heat treatment

Bacteria in water or soil can survive for days, months, even years. If feces are going to be used for fertilizer, they need to be heated to kill the bacteria. If untreated feces or urine are used, some bacteria will be killed by the heat of the sun, but some may survive, especially on root vegetables – like carrots and potatoes – which are not exposed to sun.

A good fuel – *Yemen*

Yemen is a land of burning sun. Yasmin lives in a tall old apartment house in the city of Sanaa. On the ninth floor, where her family lives, there is a toilet but no bathroom. Once a week Yasmin goes to the public bath-house to wash. After she uses the toilet she washes her bottom with a jug of water kept handy, and dries herself over the little charcoal fire that burns in a bucket next to the toilet. The toilet separates the feces and urine. There is a hole for the feces to drop down. The urine and rinsing water run over the grooved sloping floor and out through a decorative stone spout in the outside wall of the house. The liquid runs down the wall, but the sun is so hot, it usually evaporates before it reaches the ground.

Feces from all the toilets in the apartment house collect in one large container on the ground floor. Every day a man empties the container and takes the contents to the bath-house. There, he spreads the feces on the roof. The hot sun quickly dries it out. Because there is not much firewood in

Yemen, the hard dried feces (as well as scrap bones and skin from the slaughter yards) are used as fuel for fires.

Recycled effluent

People who have kitchen, bathroom and laundry taps, washing machines and flushing toilets waste a huge amount of water – 99.9 per cent of sewage is just water. In countries where water is scarce, like Israel, South Africa and America, water is recycled. Even in some parts of Australia recycled water which has been chlorinated is used to water vineyards, golf courses and vegetable crops. Effluent is good for fertilizer because it contains nutrients.

> 99.9% of sewage is water

However, it is expensive to treat effluent so it can be re-used. Most of it is just released as waste into oceans or rivers – creating health risks for swimmers and wildlife. Each year, manufacturers are asked to redesign toilets and washing machines to use less water. In 1983, a toilet flush used 2 gallons. Nowadays, a full flush uses 1½ gallons and toilets are made with half-flushes that require less than a gallon.

So much sewage!

Countries with huge water-based sewerage systems end up with tons of sewage and millions of gallons of effluent that have to be processed and disposed of.

UNPLUGGED!
Down the Plughole

> **ODD SPOT**
> Imagine sitting on the toilet, when suddenly – boom! – it explodes! That's what happened to several residents in a New York apartment block in 1996. Experts say it might have been due to a problem with water pressure in the new water-saving design. Exploding toilets are a pretty drastic way to save water!

An Australian company called Environment Equipment has developed a toilet that looks normal, but empties into a plastic compost bin instead of a sewer. The bin is under the floor on a rotating turntable. When it is full, you turn the base to position a fresh bin under the toilet…the same principle as the double vault latrines on pages 60–1. Heat, oxygen, time, and the natural bacteria in the feces are all that is needed to make the bin contents turn into safe compost. Heat, provided by electricity or a solar system, also evaporates off the liquid which is drained into an outer container. Air is drawn in through an intake hole…and smells are vented out through a pipe with the help of a fan. These 'Rota-loos' have at least six bins. By the time they are all full, the first should be ready to use as compost. If not, you can take it out, replace it with a spare bin, and leave it composting.

With a conventional flushing toilet, one person creates about 8 tons of waste a year (including water), which has to be treated, and serves no useful purpose. Using a Rota-loo, a person produces only 44 pounds of waste per year, and this is turned into fertilizer. Rota-loos have not yet appeared in private homes around Australia, but they have been installed in many National Parks, and are becoming popular overseas...especially in places where no plumbing is available.

In Sweden, many homes do use a compost latrine, called a 'Multrum', which empties into a huge fiberglass tank. Organic rubbish, like vegetable peelings, garden trimmings and meat bones can also be put into the Multrum. The composted material at the bottom of the tank can be lifted out through a trapdoor.

ODD SPOT
In the early 1800s they didn't know about having air vents in sewer pipes. One day, a plumber was asked to fix a problem with a blocked sewer pipe. He went down to the cellar carrying a bucket of water, and a candle to light his way. As he lifted up the flagstones to reveal the pipes, there was a huge bang. The candle flared up in a sheet of flame and the plumber was blown to the ground. The water bucket split in half, and the cellar door slammed shut. There was methane gas in the sewer pipe. Luckily, the plumber was more shaken than hurt.

UNPLUGGED!
Down the Plughole

Cooking with dung

When dung is placed in an airtight container, bacteria will break it down and produce a gas. This gas, called methane, is flammable. Farmers in some hot tropical countries produce their cooking gas this way, using cow dung. One cow produces about 22 pounds of dung a day. This makes just the right amount of methane to cook the farmer's meals!

Building with dung

Cow dung is also useful for building. If you're making a simple hut out of sticks and mud, like the early Australian settlers, cow dung in the mud makes the walls stronger. In Nepal the bamboo houses are coated with red mud, which the women smear on fresh every morning. They keep the edges strong by mixing in fresh green cow dung... with their hands.

Secrets in the cesspool

Cesspools were garbage dumps as well as toilets, and yesterday's garbage is today's treasure! A hundred years later, the old cesspools are dried up and free of disease. Archaeologists (people who are nutty about history) dig eagerly in old cesspools looking for treasures like broken cups and bowls, china dolls, glass drink bottles, ink bottles, and little lead soldiers.

There are even scientists, called Scatologists, who analyze the dried up old poo in cesspools to find out what people used to eat! They also examine fossilized animal dung to find out about extinct animals.

6 Making Bubbles

Solutions for cleaning teeth, hair and other bits and pieces

Soap Suds

> **MAKE YOUR OWN SOAP**
> *You will need:*
> 1 adult to help you
> 11 pounds beef fat
> a huge saucepan
> 2¾ gallons water
> cheese cloth for straining
> 1 tablespoon salt
> 1 pound caustic soda (a strong
>   alkali – be really careful)
> safety glasses
> rubber gloves
> apron or smock

To make tallow (purified fat):
Cut the fat into pieces, place in saucepan and cook on low heat. When melted, strain through cloth, squeezing out as much as possible. Pour the melted fat and 2¼ gallons of water into the

UNPLUGGED!
Making Bubbles

saucepan. This should be 1 part fat to 2 parts water. Add a tablespoon of salt.

Bring to the boil and simmer for 10 minutes, stirring. When this liquid cools, the fat forms a hard lump on top of the water. Lift it off, and scrape any rubbish off the underside.

To make soap:
In the saucepan, mix 1 pound of caustic soda into 4 pints of cold water. Warning: caustic soda burns. Be careful not to splash it on you. Heat gently over low heat and stir till caustic soda dissolves. Cool slightly. Carefully add 5 pounds of the tallow.

> Warning: caustic soda *burns*

Bring to boil over low heat, and keep boiling till it's the consistency of thick pea soup. Pour into moulds, cover with cardboard, and leave to set. After a week you can tip the soap out of the moulds, but wait a couple of months before you use it.

For vegetarians who do not want to use animal products, soap can be made from vegetable oils such as coconut, olive and palm oil.

Origins of soap

Have you ever wondered how people discovered that mixing certain ingredients makes something useful? For instance, how on earth did someone work out that mixing animal fat with an alkali makes a great cleaning substance? There is a legend to explain it.

Centuries ago, people used to sacrifice animals to their gods. According to the legend, villagers would weave their way up the winding track to their temple high up on the mountain. With songs and prayers to the gods, a young lamb or goat was placed on the altar and offered as a sacrifice. The people gave thanks for the harvest and prayed that their animals and crops would grow strong and healthy in the coming year. Then they would build a fire, roast the sacrifice, and eat it. Later, the rain would wash the animal fat and ashes down the mountain side to the river below. The women from the village found that this was the best part of the river to do their washing. Here, the water would foam and clean their clothes.

Why was this so? Alkali could have been made by water running through ashes from the fire. It must have mixed with the fat and made soap.

There are ancient Roman descriptions of making soap from goat fat and wood ash that date back 2000 years, but soap was not made in England till the 1300s.

> ...soap so strong it removed skin...

The first English soaps came in two types: expensive hard cakes for the rich, or soft liquid mush for the poor (which was so strong it removed skin as well as dirt).

Up until 1853, English soap manufacturers had to pay tax according to the amount of soap they made. In the 1500s, the tax men put locked lids on the manufacturers' boiling pans every

77

UNPLUGGED!
Making Bubbles

evening so they couldn't make extra soap in secret. Naturally, this raised the price of soap. In 1562, the price of a cake of soap was the same as a whole day's pay for a farm worker. Most people couldn't afford to buy it. Those who wanted soap had to make their own. This was not easy. They had to make the alkali by soaking wood ash or burnt seaweed. If they put too much alkali in their soap mixture, the soap burnt their skin. On the other hand, it they didn't put in enough, the meat fat in the soap went bad and stunk! This was one of the reasons washing was unpopular.

Soap was introduced to Japan in the 1500s. Before that, the Japanese rubbed themselves clean with ash or pumice stone.

After the plagues and diseases people had suffered, it became evident that it was healthier to keep clean. At the end of the First World War, the government of Aurora, Illinois, declared that people who didn't bathe at least once a week would be jailed. After centuries of discouragement from bathing, a Cleanliness Institute sprang up to promote washing. This was a boon for the soap manufacturers. Suddenly there were not just great varieties of soaps, but bubble baths, bath soaps, bath salts and bath oils too.

Hair care

In the 1600s, wigs for men were the fashion, because it was easier to shave off hair than wash it. In the 1700s, women had elaborate hairstyles intertwining their real hair with wigs on wire frames. This was styled with pomade (a mixture of apple juice and pig fat) and whitened with flour (white hair was fashionable). Naturally, this concoction couldn't be brushed, let alone washed. Once a week a maid would check the hair and try to catch all the nits and fleas attracted by the pomade. About three times a year, ladies would let their hair down to wash it with wood ash and water. Men also whitened their hair with flour. This absorbed some of the oil in their hair, so when they brushed it out they got rid of some dirt and grease.

During the 1800s, fashion changed completely. Girls were taught to brush their hair with a hundred strokes every night. Women made their own shampoos and conditioners.

...brush with a hundred strokes...

The usual ingredients were alkali and egg. Men plastered their hair down with a grease called Macassar Oil. Servants put little lace cloths on the backs of armchairs so the upholstery wouldn't be stained by the hair oil. These cloths were named anti-macassars.

Commercial shampoos appeared this century.

Pearly whites

People living in the African country of Zaire take great pride in having pearly white teeth. The

UNPLUGGED!
Making Bubbles

traditional way to clean teeth there is with a willow twig frayed at the end.

The ancient Romans cleaned their teeth by chewing sap from the mastic tree. They had solid silver toothpicks, and used mouthwashes to keep their teeth white.

Toothbrushes were not commonly used in England until the 1850s. Up until then, a grinning face was an ugly sight, by our standards. Teeth were either yellow or black.

> ...teeth were yellow or black...

People made homemade tooth cleaners out of things like soot, tobacco, honey, sugar, fruit peel, brick dust or cuttlefish bones (which ate into the enamel of the teeth and made them rot more!). Instead of toothbrushes, people used a linen cloth, a frayed stick, or a piece of root from a hollyhock flower. Some people tried to grind off the stains with pumice stone, or powder from pounded-up bricks or coral. Alternatively, they rinsed with a tooth whitener made of lemon juice, salt and alum. To hide the bad breath caused by decaying teeth and diseased gums, they used a mouthwash made from cinnamon, cloves, honey, orange peel or wine.

Facials

Hundreds of years ago, when hygiene was not what it is today, people caught dreadful diseases like smallpox, which left horrible pockmarks in the skin. Women tried all sorts of tricks to improve or hide their awful complexions. Some of the face cleaners included ingredients like animal dung, puppy dog urine, ass's milk and goat hair, as well as more normal things like herbs, flower petals, lemon juice and cucumbers. Some women had great faith in mercury water, not realizing that if they used it too often it would actually eat into their skin and make scars. When all else failed, the solution was to hide bad blemishes with small black cloth patches stuck on the face. These became fashionable and were actually called beauty spots!

English fashion in the 1500s demanded white skin. Rich women painted their faces, neck and arms with a cosmetic called ceruse. This contained

UNPLUGGED!
Making Bubbles

white lead, which was not only poisonous but tended to make open sores on their skin!

In the 1700s, high foreheads were considered beautiful. Women plucked out their hair, and put a mixture of cat dung and vinegar on their foreheads to stop the hair growing back!

In the name of beauty

We laugh now at the things people used to put on themselves in the name of beauty. But do you know anything about the ingredients of modern lotions and make-up? Many moisturizers contain things like hyaluronic acid, elastin, collagen and ambergris which come from whales, rooster combs and other animals. Where once white skin was fashionable, being suntanned became all important. In 1990 a whole lot of self-tanning lotions and moisturizers had to be banned because it was discovered that one ingredient (urocanic acid) could be linked to cancer. Now we are very conscious of being 'sun smart'.

The modern beauty image is created by stars on TV and movie screens, and by advertising photographs in magazines. They set up an ideal of a slim

...modern beauty image...

hairless body with unblemished and unwrinkled skin. Trying to achieve this ideal, modern women do strange things like having all the hair on their legs ripped out (waxing), or peeling skin off their faces with acid treatments.

Body odor

When washing was not the routine, people had to cover themselves and their clothes with strong scents. One solution was rubbing the skin with rose petals. Grand houses in England had a special room for making perfumes from roses and from other flowers and herbs. The recipes for these were passed down from older generations.

Going outdoors, people wanted strong perfumes to block out the dreadful smells from sewage lying around – especially because they believed the bad smells spread disease. They poured oil of rosemary or other herbs on hankies to hold to their noses. Eau de Cologne was invented because it was thought it might be a protection against the plague.

Nowadays, we have fewer problems with smells from unwashed bodies or sewage, but we have an endless choice of commercial perfumes and deodorants for every part of the body.

> ...an endless choice of deodorants...

UNPLUGGED!

7 Care for a Dust Bath?

Animal hygiene

Dirty beasts?

If a horse, zebra or bison is living in a hot dry place, he cleans himself by rolling in dust or sand. Then he stands up and shakes himself. Deer, pigs and rhinos enjoy a good mud bath to clean off dead hair and parasites. Deer puddle up the mud first with their hooves. Afterwards, they rub themselves against tree trunks or rocks, tip their heads back and scratch themselves with their horns or antlers. By the time they finish scratching and rubbing, they are shiny and clean.

Pigs and rhinos, on the other hand, like to keep on a coating of mud. This makes them look 'like dirty pigs' but it actually has a purpose. If there is no protective coating of mud, parasites bite them, lay eggs and burrow into their skin. The mud also keeps them feeling cool while the water evaporates. An elephant likes to wash in water, but when he comes out he will 'powder' himself with dust or sand. His skin looks tough, but it is actually quite delicate.

Some birds clean themselves with dust. They

squirm and flutter in the dust bath just as if it were water. They rub in the dust with their beaks and claws. Then they shake it out, rearrange and preen their feathers.

The preeners

Birds are very cleverly designed to produce their own cleaning products. When they want to clean their feathers, water birds and most other birds just have to dip their beaks into a special preen gland near their tails. This gland supplies oil for waterproofing feathers. Water birds have microscopically small spikes on their feathers which need to be oiled to stay flexible. In the water, the birds fluff out their feathers and the spikes keep the water away from their bodies so they don't get too cold. But if birds are caught in an oil spill from ships, the oil coats them and stops their feathers from working.

UNPLUGGED!
Care for a Dust Bath?

Before oiling themselves, birds wash in water, and dry their feathers by squeezing them with their beaks and flapping their wings.

Other birds also use preen gland oil to make themselves waterproof in case of rain. Some birds, like herons and parrots, produce powder instead of oil. You've probably seen birds splashing in puddles or flying through sprinklers. Birds love to wash, but they always preen afterwards. If they have trouble with hard-to-reach parts, like the neck, they fluff out their feathers and a friendly neighbor will preen it for them.

UNSOLVED MYSTERY
Why do birds use ants for beauty treatments? Some birds deliberately sit on ant nests and let the ants crawl all over them. Birds like crows, ravens, starlings and blackbirds even go so far as to pick ants up with their beaks and wipe them onto their feathers. Ants release formic acid, and maybe this acts as a pleasant skin lotion or kills skin parasites (formic acid is an insecticide), but bird observers are only guessing.

Eating their own dirt

When you see monkeys picking at themselves, they are not looking for fleas. They are looking for tasty bits of dandruff, dead skin, scabs or dirt to eat! This is one way to keep clean. Monkeys also groom each other as a sign of friendship. They will even pick dirt out of each other's teeth! To do this they sometimes strip leaves off little twigs to make toothpicks. Monkeys also use twigs to clean their beards and eyebrows. They say if you want to calm an angry monkey, you should give it a gentle pat. It will probably lie down and wait to be groomed.

Getting licked

What would you do if you were frightened and there was nowhere to run to for safety? Would you scream? Would you attack? If you were a rat you'd stand up on your hind legs and lick yourself clean! Rats are obsessed with cleaning themselves, and if they have nothing else to do they start licking and combing. Naturalist Phil Drabble describes their odd behavior in his book *A Weasel in my Meat Safe*.

Many animals use their tongues for cleaning. You've seen cats do it. Mother cats lick their babies clean, and even wash their bottoms for them. Rats and mice lick their front paws and then wipe their faces, whiskers and ears. Some use the long toes on their back paws like Q-tips – cleaning inside their ears and licking off the dirt. Rabbits lick their paws clean to make sure they can run fast. The oil in rabbits' ears absorbs vitamin D from exposure to the sun. When they wipe their ears with their paws, and then lick the paws, they get a dose of vitamin D. This helps

UNPLUGGED!
Care for Dust Bath?

protect them from a disease called rickets.

Buffaloes lick their lips and nostrils clean. Small

> ...lick their nostrils clean

giraffes, called okapis, have such long tongues they can lick their eyes clean!

A mother kangaroo prepares for the birth of a baby by holding open her pouch and licking it – for a couple of hours! When the tiny naked baby appears from the birth canal, she keeps licking it with her tongue to keep it moist as it works its way into the pouch.

Insects lick themselves clean. If dirt catches in their tiny joints it will breed diseases. They take special care to keep their eyes clean. Next time you see a fly resting, watch it. You will probably see it cleaning its head, body and wings. Bees have special combs built into their front legs so they can clean their antennae. They brush the pollen off their bodies into built-in baskets on their back legs.

Fishy housekeepers

Some fish provide a cleaning service for other underwater creatures. A snorkler may be surprised to find a Wrasse fish nibbling the moles off his back! Most cleaner

> ...one fish can clean 300...

fish are recognizable by their bright coloring.

When they see a possible customer, they wriggle and make little nibbling movements to attract attention. Often, they have one special place where they 'keep shop' – perhaps a distinctive rock or coral. Sometimes there is a line of customers! One fish can clean as many as 300 customers in six hours. The customer usually relaxes and keeps still while the cleaner nibbles him all over, removing tiny crustaceans or furry white bacterial growth from wounds. The cleaner fish taps for fins to be raised, or mouths to be opened. Tiny Wrasse can go inside the mouth of a large aggressive fish like a barracuda to clean his teeth for him – and not get eaten. The big fish snaps his jaws a few times to show when he's had enough, but he doesn't swallow the cleaner.

Schools of Labeo Vellifer fish, each 1½ feet long, use their suckers to latch onto hippos so they can clean them. The tropical angel fish is nicknamed the 'barber' because it does such a good grooming job. Some fish travel long distances for a clean.

> **ODD SPOT**
> There are a few animals and birds that act as cleaners. The most amazing is the Egyptian plover bird which actually cleans the teeth of the Nile crocodile!

There are also cleaner shrimps, who clean larger sea creatures like lobsters. They even clean the gigantic and greedy Moray eels. Lobsters and shrimps clean their own delicate antennae by rubbing them with their pincers or between their legs. They need clean antennae so they can feel their way and feed at night.

UNPLUGGED!
Care for A Dust Bath?

Disposable skin

Snakes have it easy. They just shed their old dirty skins, and have clean new ones ready underneath. The snake rubs its face against a rock to split the old skin, then glides forward as the old skin peels off inside out (just like you pulling your socks off?). If the skin doesn't come off cleanly, the snake keeps rubbing to scrape off the bits.

Crabs have a hard upper body shell that they can throw away when they need to grow a new bigger one.

Toilet stop

Humans urinate or defecate to get rid of waste from their bodies. Animals have other reasons as well. Rhinos, hippos and dogs mark out their territory using urine or feces. Hippos actually use the brush on the end of their tails to splatter the dung right round their area. Zdenek Veselovsky, in his book *Are Animals Different?*, describes how his pet Slow Loris urinated on its hands and feet and then rubbed this moisture on everything it took a fancy to (including the clothes in Veselovsky's wardrobe). When its cage was cleaned out, it had extra drinks so it could re-mark its territory. (The Slow Loris is a thick-furred tree-climbing animal, related to the monkey.)

When a baby koala is hungry, the mother koala has the amazing ability to pass partly digested leaves out of her anus, instead of feces!

Some animals, such as deer, cattle, monkeys and birds, just defecate or urinate where and when they feel like it. Others, like rabbits, rhinos and llamas, have a special place that their whole group uses as a communal toilet. Cats and badgers actually go one step further and cover up their droppings with earth.

A nest is a rather small crowded home, and it wouldn't be very pleasant if it were full of droppings. Most baby nesting birds conveniently deposit their droppings neatly packaged in a clean jelly-like wrapping. The parents just have to pick it up in their beaks and carry it away from the nest. Lyrebirds sometimes dig holes to bury these packages in. Young birds of prey, such as eagles and hawks, save their parents the trouble of cleaning up. They are clever enough to lift their bottoms up and squirt their droppings out of the nest. Hooded Parrots of the Australian Northern Territory allow caterpillars to share their nest, and the caterpillars keep the nest clean by eating the droppings!

Doggy doos

Many people take their dogs for walks to leave squishy brown presents on other people's front lawns or nature strips. This is not cool! In Australia, many local councils have made this inconsiderate habit illegal, and dog owners can be fined hundreds of dollars. Some councils provide

UNPLUGGED!
Care for A Dust Bath?

dog toilets in parks, usually a hole in the ground with chemicals in it, that you're supposed to drop the droppings in. Pet shops and councils sell scoopers made of plastic, metal or cardboard for picking up your dog's little gift and putting it in a plastic bag or dog toilet.

In Paris, mini cleaning trucks drive constantly around the sidewalks. A large vacuum hose hangs out the front, looking like an elephant trunk. The driver bobs it up and down to pick up dog droppings and other garbage.

In the tiny village of Bruntingthorpe in Britain, people got so sick of dog doo everywhere that they decided to call on forensic science to find the culprits. The scientists took sample hairs from the 30 dogs in the village. These hairs were analyzed to find out each dog's DNA – the chemical code that identifies every bit of that one dog. Now if any dropping appears on the street, scientists can examine it, find out the DNA and identify the guilty dog!

Glossary

cholera	an infectious disease of the intestines, with severe vomiting and diarrhea
coronation	ceremony to crown a king or queen
crustacean	certain animals with hard outer 'shells' such as shrimps, lobsters and crabs
etiquette	rules of polite behavior
halfpenny	small British coin, the value of half a penny
hepatitis	severe disease of the liver
irrigation	a system of supplying water to crops, often by the use of canals
mercury	poisonous liquid metal, often used in thermometers
parasite	an animal or plant that gets food by living on something else, e.g. lice and fleas
paratyphoid	similar to typhoid but less severe
plague	usually refers to bubonic plague, a highly infectious disease causing blood poisoning, and usually death
potpourri	mixture of scented flowers and leaves
rickets	a disease which prevents bones from hardening so that they bend out of shape
sultan	the royal leader of a Muslim country
typhoid	a serious infectious disease, with fever and inflamed intestines
whooping cough	an infectious disease with a noisy cough

UNPLUGGED!

Further reading

Switch! Home-based power, water and sewerage systems for the twenty-first century by Jackie French and Brian Sullivan
(Aird Books, Melbourne, 1994)

The Bath by Diane Von Furstenberg
(Random House, New York, 1993)

Wash and Brush Up by Eleanor Allen
(Adam and Charles Black, London, 1976)

Sanitation without water by Uno Winblad and Wen Kilama
(Macmillan, London, 1985)

Animal Activities: Keeping Clean by Jane Burton
(Belitha, London, 1989)

Hygiene by Don Nardo
(Chelsea House, New York, 1993)

The Complete Soapmaker by Norma Coney
(Sterling, New York, 1995)

Cotswold Privies by Mollie Harris
(Chatto and Windus, London, 1984)

Index

Africa 44, 52–4, 71, 79
America 39, 48, 52, 71
animals 74, 77, 82, 84–9
aqueduct 23, 26
Asia 44, 48, 52
Australia 12, 44, 64, 65, 71, 72–3, 91–2

bacteria 37, 45–50, 53, 54, 65, 70, 73
Bangladesh 57–8
baths 21–36, 39, 70, 78
Bhutan 58–9, 60

cesspool 10, 12, 17, 37, 62, 74
chamberpot 9, 10–12, 17, 38, 66
China 48, 67, 69
commode 10–12
compost toilet 60, 69, 72–3
Crapper, Thomas 15

disease 37–50, 53-4, 80, 83, 88

England 8–9, 10–11, 27, 39–40, 41, 77, 80, 83

fleas 37, 40, 41, 48, 49, 79
flush 14–16, 19, 59–61, 71
France 12, 40–41, 92

germs 37, 47, 54, 61

hair 21, 40, 41, 78–9, 82
hip bath 28–30

Japan 8, 12–13, 32–3, 62, 78

lice 40, 47
Lister, Lord 46
London 9, 26–7, 31–2, 38, 42–3, 45
long drop toilet 52

Melbourne 28–30, 43–5, 62–4
methane 73

Nepal 54–7, 74
nightcart 62–4

UNPLUGGED!
Index

Pasteur, Louis 46–7
pit toilet 13–14, 52–3, 61
plumbing 24, 45, 54, 64
privy 12, 43, 62–3
public toilet 8, 9, 15, 18

sewage systems 37, 65, 71–2
shampoo 41, 79
soap 16, 67, 75–8
Sweden 73

toothbrush 80

Vietnam 52–4, 60

water cart 29–30

Yemen 70–71